Everyday Inventions

Inventions We Use for
Information and Entertainment

Jane Bidder

GARETH**STEVENS**
PUBLISHING
A Member of the WRC Media Family of Companies

Please visit our web site at: www.garethstevens.com
For a free color catalog describing Gareth Stevens Publishing's list of
high-quality books and multimedia programs, call 1-800-542-2595 (USA) or
1-800-387-3178 (Canada). Gareth Stevens Publishing's fax: (414) 332-3567.

Library of Congress Cataloging-in-Publication Data

Bidder, Jane.
    Inventions we use for information and entertainment / by Jane Bidder.
       p. cm. — (Everyday inventions)
    Includes bibliographical references and index.
    ISBN-10: 0-8368-6899-4 — ISBN-13: 978-0-8368-6899-9 (lib. bdg.)
    1. Information technology—Juvenile literature. 2. Amusements—Technological
innovations—Juvenile literature. 3. Inventions—Juvenile literature. I. Title.
    T58.5.B485   2006
    621.382—dc22   2006004290

This North American edition first published in 2007 by
Gareth Stevens Publishing
A Member of the WRC Media Family of Companies
330 West Olive Street, Suite 100
Milwaukee, WI 53212 USA

This U.S. edition copyright © 2007 by Gareth Stevens, Inc. Original edition copyright © 2006 by Franklin Watts.
First published in Great Britain in 2006 by Franklin Watts, 338 Euston Road, London NW1 3BH, United Kingdom.

Watts series editor: Jennifer Schofield
Watts art director: Jonathan Hair
Watts designer: Ross George
Watts picture researcher: Diana Morris
Watts artwork: Ray Bryant
Gareth Stevens editors: Tea Benduhn and Barbara Kiely Miller
Gareth Stevens art direction: Tammy West
Gareth Stevens graphic designer: Dave Kowalski

Acknowledgements: The author would like to thank Marry Bellis of inventors.about.com.
for her help in researching this book.

Picture credits (t=top, b=bottom, l=left, r=right, c=center): AKG Images: 10t, 14bl, 19. Alex Bartel/SPL: 7b.
Bettmann/CORBIS: 16b, 21, 23t, 27b. British Library/HIP Topfoto: 7t. CORBIS: 18bl. Steve Crise/CORBIS: 11.
Julio Donoso/Sygma/CORBIS: 26. Alexander Farnsworth/IW/Topfoto: 23b. LWA-JDC/CORBIS: 24. Mary Evans
Picture Library: 10b, 12b. Museum of London/HIP/Topfoto: 9c. Richard T. Nowitz/CORBIS: 27t. Phillips: 4t,
12t, 20t, 22t. Picturepoint/Topfoto: 9b, 22b. Louie Psihoyos/CORBIS: 25. RNT Productions/CORBIS: 18tr.
Roger-Viollet/Topfoto: 20b.

Printed in the United States of America

1 2 3 4 5 6 7 8 9 10 09 08 07 06

Contents

Words that appear in the glossary are
printed in **boldface** type the first
time they occur in the text.

About Inventions

An invention is a **device** or a tool that is designed and made for the first time. The person who designs the device is called an inventor. This book looks at some of the inventions that help people stay in contact with each other and communicate their ideas and thoughts. It also introduces inventors and shows how inventions we use for information and entertainment have changed over time.

Easy Living

People invented many ways to communicate because they wanted to improve their lives or make them easier. Ballpoint pens, for example, are not as messy as fountain pens. After ballpoint pens were invented, in 1938, people no longer had to refill their pens or accidentally spill ink on their paper — or even on themselves!

Getting It Right the First Time

Sometimes, inventors have ideas and **develop** those ideas until their inventions work. In 1827, for example, French scientist Joseph Niépce worked with light so he could find a quick way to capture images. Niépce found a way to capture images when he made the first camera and developed the first photograph.

From One Comes Another

The final design of an invention is not always the same as the first. Many inventions change and improve over time. The first telephones, for example, had separate wires for each telephone they could "talk" to. Later, the **telephone exchange** was invented, but an **operator** had to connect each call. Now people can make direct calls to almost anywhere in the world.

TIME LINE

You will find time lines throughout this book. Use these time lines to keep track of when things happened.

The time lines show, in date order, when specific breakthroughs occurred or particular inventions were introduced. Sometimes, the dates are very exact, but other times, they point to particular eras or decades, such as "the 1990s."

The Printed Word

People read and write every day, but the written word has not always been a part of daily life. People

invented writing in Mesopotamia (now Iraq) about 5,500 years ago. Writing has changed since that time. Today, people write on paper instead of on clay or stone, and they have ways to print words with machines.

Wood-Block Printing

In about A.D. 700, the Chinese invented wood-block printing. People carved letters out of blocks of wood. Then they covered the surfaces of the wood-block letters with ink and pressed the blocks onto paper to "print" the letters on the page.

Making Paper
In 2500 B.C., Egyptians made paper from **papyrus** reeds, which they gathered from river banks. Today, paper is made mostly from wood pulp.

Printing Press

Through the **Middle Ages**, people copied books by hand. Then, in Germany, in 1440, Johann Gutenberg invented a printing press that could print about three thousand pages a day. To print a page, people known as printers arranged metal letters, line by line, covered the letters with ink, and then pressed them onto paper.

Today's Printing Presses

Today, many printing presses use a method of printing called lithography. Lithography uses large, flat printing blocks to press words and pictures onto paper. The biggest presses can print, trim, and fold eighty thousand copies of a ninety-six page newspaper in one hour.

TIME LINE

3500 B.C.
People in Mesopotamia invent writing.

A.D. 700
The Chinese print with wood blocks.

1040-1050
The Chinese invent moveable type.

1400
Europeans learn how to print with wood blocks.

1440
Gutenberg invents the printing press and prints a Bible.

1798
Austrian actor and playwright Alois Senefelder develops lithographic printing.

1971
Xerox, in California, makes the first laser printer.

Postal Service

Each day, all over the world, postal workers deliver letters and packages to people's homes. The postal service, however, is not new. It started as long ago as 2000 B.C., in ancient Egypt.

Royal Post

King Louis XI of France started the first modern postal service in 1464. In 1516, Henry VIII of England set up a postal service for the delivery of royal mail. Messengers and young postboys carried government letters.

Mailboxes

The first street mailboxes were not very successful. People often put their trash in the mailboxes, instead of their mail, which attracted rats!

Then, in 1627, the French government allowed the public to use the mail service. In 1635, the English government allowed the public to use the royal mail service.

Mail Coaches

Mail coaches replaced messengers and postboys in 1784. Horse-drawn coaches moved faster and carried more mail than people on horseback or foot. In the 1850s, across the United States, relay stations allowed coaches to change horses.

Stamps

In 1840, in England, Sir Rowland Hill came up with the idea of using a stamp to cover the cost of postage. Seven years later, the United States government issued its first postage stamps. The 5-cent stamp had a picture of Benjamin Franklin on it to honor his role as the first Postmaster General. Today, people collect stamps from all over the world.

TIME LINE

2000 B.C.
Ancient Egyptians deliver written messages.

A.D. 1464
King Louis XI starts a postal service in France.

1516
Henry VIII sets up a royal mail service in England.

1784
High-speed coaches carry the mail in the United States and England.

1840
England's Sir Rowland Hill invents the first postage stamp.

1860
In the United States, the Pony Express postal service is established to deliver mail more quickly to the western states.

Electric Telegraph

The electric telegraph was a communication system that sent messages by means of an electric pulse traveling through wires. For many years, people used telegraphs to send messages to soldiers at war and to ships at sea.

A Code That Worked

The telegraph used pulses of electricity to create a series of dots and dashes that printed on a roll of paper at the receiving end. In 1835, Samuel Morse and Alfred Vail developed a system for the dots and dashes to represent letters and numbers that could be decoded. The system, called Morse code, was later adopted worldwide.

The First Telegraph Message

Morse and Vail made improvements to their first telegraph machine. In 1838, they gave a public **demonstration** of their improved telegraph machine. Five years later, they started building a telegraph wire that linked Washington, D.C., to Baltimore, Maryland, 40 miles (65 kilometers) away. On May 24, 1844, Morse sent his first message which was, "What hath God wrought."

Using Telegraph Lines

In 1845, people started using telegraph lines to also send telegrams. Telegrams were printed telegraph messages, which special message carriers delivered as fast as possible. Western Union, the best-known telegraph company, sent its last message in 2006.

TIME LINE

1835
Samuel Morse and Alfred Vail invent Morse code.

1844
Morse and Vail send the first telegraph message.

1845
People use telegraph wires to send telegrams.

1851
Western Union Telegraph Company is established in North America.

1861
Western Union builds a telegraph line across the whole country.

1970s
E-mail begins to replace telegraph messages.

2006
Western Union sends the final telegraph message.

Telephones

Today, across the world, there are millions of landline and wireless telephones in use. When the telephone was first invented, however, people were not sure it would even be useful.

Marvelous Meucci

Many people think that Alexander Graham Bell invented the first telephone in 1876. In 1849, however, Italian-born inventor Antonio Meucci (*right*) discovered that sound could travel through copper wire. Around 1860, he developed a working model for the telephone. Alexander Graham Bell developed a similar idea and filed a **patent** in 1876 for the first telephone.

The Telephone Exchange

The first telephones needed an operator to connect one caller to another. Almon Strowger, a Kansas City businessman, thought the operators were connecting his callers to his **rivals**, so, in 1891, he invented the automatic telephone exchange. The exchange allowed people to dial a direct connection without going through an operator.

Mobile Madness

In 1946, police officers tested the first mobile telephones in their cars. In 1968, telephone companies saw that other people would also want mobile phones, so they began to develop the technology. As mobile phones became less expensive and more efficient, they also became more common.

TIME LINE

1849
Antonio Meucci discovers that sound can travel through copper wire.

1876
Alexander Graham Bell patents a telephone.

1891
Almon Strowger invents the first direct-dial telephone exchange.

1946
Police test the first mobile telephones in their cars.

2000s
Mobile phones can operate in **isolated** areas, such as remote parts of Africa.

Mobile phones can be used to take pictures, send text messages, listen to music, browse the Internet, play games, watch video, and more.

Pens

Using a pen to write on a piece of paper is one of the easiest ways to get a message to someone, to make a note, and to record information. Today, pens come in many sizes with different types of ink, but this variety was not always available.

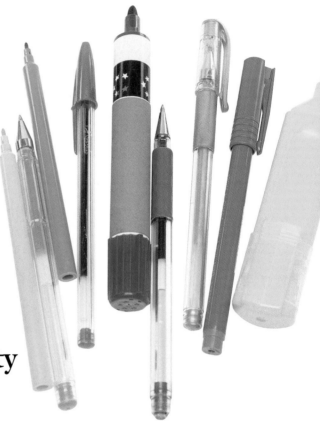

Quill Pens

As long ago as A.D. 600, people living in Europe made pens from the feathers of large birds. They sharpened the tips of the feathers' quills to make fine points and then dipped the quills in ink to write with. People used quill pens for more than one thousand years.

Fountain Pens

A fountain pen was the first pen to have a store of ink inside the pen that flows down to the point, or nib. In 1702, Nicholas Bion designed one of the first fountain pens for the king of France. Although Bion's pen worked better than a quill, it spilled a lot of ink. In 1884, Lewis Waterman of New York patented a pen that did not leak. The ink in Waterman's pen also flowed more evenly than Bion's.

Ballpoint Pens

In 1938, Hungarian brothers Lazlo and George Biro, invented a pen with a tiny ball at the tip. The ball helped the ink flow smoothly and gave the pen its name. Today, ballpoint pens remain one of the most popular types of pens.

TIME LINE

3000 B.C.
Egyptians write with a reed pen on papyrus.

A.D. 100
Romans write using a metal or bone stick, called a stylus, on a wax tablet.

600-1800s
People use quill pens.

1702
Nicholas Bion makes a fountain pen.

1938
The Biro brothers invent the ballpoint pen.

1962
Yukio Horie of the Tokyo Stationery Company develops a felt-tip pen.

Today
Pens come in many styles with many different colors of ink. Some ink is even invisible!

Photography

Can you imagine reading a newspaper or magazine with no photographs in it, or going on a vacation and not taking a single picture to remember it by?

The First Photograph

In 1827, French inventor Joseph Niépce made the first photograph. He attached a lens to a wooden box. Inside the box, he placed a metal plate coated with a layer of a special tar. The lens **projected** a picture onto the tar. After eight hours, the tar showed a negative of the picture. To make a positive image, Niépce washed the tar with chemicals to reveal the photograph above.

Kodak Number 1

In 1888, George Eastman of New York invented the first handheld camera, called the Kodak Number 1. The Kodak camera was easy to use and became very popular. When the preloaded roll of film was used up, people sent the whole camera to Eastman's company to print the photos.

Polaroid

In 1947, in Massachusetts, Edwin Land invented the Land Polaroid camera. The Polaroid was different from any other camera because it could instantly develop a photograph as soon as the picture was taken. At first, the cameras were very expensive. As more people bought them, they became affordable for everyone.

TIME LINE

1827
Joseph Niépce makes the first photograph.

1841
William Henry Fox Talbot invents a process for printing multiple copies from one negative image.

1861
Scottish scientist James Clerk Maxwell makes the first color photograph.

1888
George Eastman invents a handheld camera.

1947
Edwin Land invents the Land Polaroid camera.

1975
The Kodak company experiments with digital pictures.

1991
Kodak, Canon, and other companies make **digital cameras** for the public.

Cinema

Moving pictures began as long ago as 1891. The first films were silent, and the pictures were black and white. Like today's films, they worked by showing a series of still pictures so fast that the images in the pictures appeared to move.

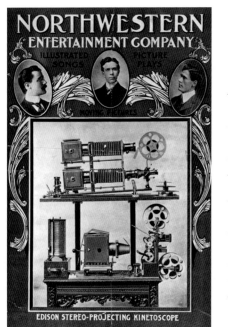

Early Beginnings

In 1891, William Dickson, who worked with Thomas Edison, made a camera that showed forty-six photographs per second. The camera had a peep hole through which Edison could see Dickson's flickering "moving" images. Dickson named his moving camera a kinetoscope, and Edison developed the kinetoscope to make a film projector.

Screen Machine

In 1895, French brothers Auguste and Louis Lumière made a light, portable camera that could take pictures, develop film, and project images. They named their invention the Cinematographe. The Lumières made many short films to show to the public.

Adding Sound and Color

At first, films were not only short but also silent and in black and white. The only sound was provided by a pianist. Then, in 1927, Warner Brothers made *The Jazz Singer*, which was one of the first films with **synchronized** sound. Audiences could now hear the actors talking and singing while the pictures moved on the screen.

TIME LINE

1891
Dickson makes the first moving pictures on film.

1895
Auguste and Louis Lumière invent the Cinematographe.

1902
French magician Georges Méliès makes the first space travel film, *A Trip to the Moon*.

1918
Leon Douglass, in California, makes a full-length color film called *Cupid Angling*.

1927
The Jazz Singer is the first film with synchronized sound.

1980s
People can rent movies to watch at home.

Radio

Have you ever wondered how information reaches your radio? A radio station sends out **radio waves** that carry information to radio receivers. Your radio turns the waves into speech or music. Then it **broadcasts** the latest news, weather, pop songs, and much more.

Marconi's Magic

The inventor who made radios possible was Italian scientist Guglielmo Marconi. In 1895, Marconi sent a Morse code message across a room without using wires. In 1901, after improving his discovery, Marconi sent the first radio message across the Atlantic Ocean, from England to Canada!

Words and Music

Marconi's invention sent Morse code messages between just two people. Then, in 1906, Canadian scientist Reginald Fessenden sent the first broadcast of words and music on radio waves, much to the surprise of the people listening for Morse code.

Radio Stations

By 1920, radio stations began to appear across the United States. RCA started the  National Broadcasting Company (NBC) in 1926. Soon, listening to the radio became a family activity. In the evenings, everyone gathered around the radio to listen to programs. One of the longest-running radio programs was *Amos and Andy*, which aired from 1928 to 1960.

TIME LINE

1861
James Clerk Maxwell starts to work with radio waves in England.

1895
Guglielmo Marconi invents equipment that sends radio waves through the air.

1901
Marconi sends a radio message across the Atlantic Ocean.

1906
Reginald Fessenden broadcasts words and music in the United States and Canada.

1920s
Radio stations appear.

1990s
Digital radio stations begin broadcasting in the United States.

2001
Apple releases the first iPod digital music player.

Television

Television provides people with both information and entertainment. A broadcasting station sends a sound signal and a picture

signal to a television set. The TV then builds the picture signal into lines across the screen. When people see the lines, their eyes make the lines join together to form a picture.

In England

In the 1920s, Scottish **engineer** John Logie Baird experimented with radio waves to see if he could send picture signals along with sound signals. In 1924, he got an outline picture of an object to appear on a screen. Two years later, he was able to demonstrate pictures that moved. By 1930, Baird made moving images with sound and color.

In the United States

In 1920, Utah teenager Philo Farnsworth drew a picture for his teacher of a device which later became the basis for all modern televisions. By 1927, Farnsworth had built the device he had drawn, and he showed a successful moving image.

Satellite Television

Satellite television became popular in the 1980s. Television stations send signals to satellites in space, which bounce signals back to satellite dishes on Earth. Today, many houses and apartments have satellite dishes that pick up television signals from space.

1920s
John Logie Baird and Philo Farnsworth work on showing pictures on a television screen.

1928
Baird sends the first television pictures from London to New York.

Baird demonstrates the first TV broadcast in color.

1940s
John and Margaret Walson start cable television in Pennsylvania.

1956
Zenith introduces a remote control.

1980s
Satellite television is available, and **98** percent of U.S. homes have at least one TV set.

1990s
High Definition Television (HDTV) starts to become popular.

The Internet

The Internet is not just one of the fastest ways to find out information. Without it, e-mail would not be possible. E-mail is one of the quickest ways to send a message to someone.

How It All Started

In 1954, the Massachusetts Institute of Technology (MIT) began a project to improve the U.S. Air Force's national defense system. Scientists developed a computer network called SAGE that linked **radar** stations across the country so they could warn each other of an attack. Later, a better computer **network**, known as **ARPANET**, linked the computers of many U.S. government departments.

Sending E-Mails

In 1971, Ray Tomlinson, an engineer at MIT, developed electronic mail or e-mail. Tomlinson used ARPANET to make a way for researchers to send each other messages. He chose the @ symbol to show which user was using which network. Today, across the world, people send and receive millions of e-mails each day to computers at offices, schools, and homes.

Web Browsing

In 1989, British computer scientist Tim Berners-Lee invented the World Wide Web. The next year, he created the first **Web browser**.

His computer program allowed people to see information on Web sites through a global computer network called the Internet.

TIME LINE

1954
The U.S. Air Force begins to network computers that act as an early warning system for attack during the **Cold War**.

Late 1960s
SAGE develops into ARPANET – an information-sharing computer program.

1971
Ray Tomlinson develops electronic mail (e-mail).

1989
Tim Berners-Lee invents the World Wide Web.

1998
Larry Page and Sergey Brin, students at Stanford University in California, create Google, one of the largest **search engines** on the Internet.

Other Inventions

Each day, many other inventions help people communicate their thoughts and ideas. People who cannot see, for example, use Braille — a series of raised dots they can feel — to read and write. Many people who have hearing difficulties use a special sign language to communicate.

Braille

There are millions of people who cannot see. In France, in 1824, a blind teenager named Louis Braille adapted a military code as a way for people who are blind to read and write. Braille is a system that uses patterns of raised dots to represent letters or words. People read by feeling the shapes of the patterns with their fingers. At first, people had to write Braille by punching dots into the paper with a stylus. In 1892, Frank Haven Hall of Illinois invented the Braille typewriter.

Signing

Sign language is a system of hand signals and facial expressions that helps people communicate.

In 1755, Abbe de L'epee of France started a school for the deaf that taught sign language. Today, there are many forms of sign language, including American Sign Language and International Sign Language.

Mechanical Telegraph

In 1792, the Chappe brothers of France invented a machine that moved a pair of wooden arms in patterns that represented letters of the alphabet. Their invention, called a semaphore, allowed visual messages to be sent from the signal station. Railroads use semaphores to communicate, and people can act as semaphores with handheld flags.

ALPHABETS

In the 11th century B.C., the Phoenicians, who lived around the Mediterranean, made a simple alphabet that did not have vowels. In about 900 B.C., the Greeks added vowels to the Phoenician alphabet.

Later, the Etruscans, one of the earliest civilizations in Italy, and the Romans improved the Greek alphabet to make the alphabet that many modern languages use today.

Time Line

3500 B.C.
The Mesopotamians invent the first writing system.

900 B.C.
The Greeks add vowels to the Phoenician alphabet.

A.D. 600 – 1800
People use quill pens.

700
The Chinese print with wood blocks.

1440
Gutenberg invents a printing press that uses moveable type.

1464
King Louis XI starts a postal service in France.

1755
Abbe de L'Epee of France starts a school for the deaf.

1798
Austrian actor Alois Senefelder develops lithographic printing.

1824
Braille is invented in France.

1827
Joseph Niépce of France makes the first photograph.

1835
Samuel Morse and Alfred Vail invent Morse code.

1845
People use telegraph wires to send telegrams.

1861
In England, James Clerk Maxwell works with radio waves. He also makes the first color photograph.

1876
Alexander Graham Bell develops Antonio Meucci's idea and patents a telephone.

1888
George Eastman invents a handheld camera.

1891
Almon Strowger invents a direct-dial telephone exchange.

William Dickson makes the first moving pictures on film.

1895
Guglielmo Marconi sends radio waves.

1906
Canadian Reginald Fessenden broadcasts radio words and music.

1920s
John Logie Baird and Philo Farnsworth work on showing pictures on a television screen.

1927
The Jazz Singer is the first film with synchronized sound.

1928
John Logie Baird sends television pictures from London to New York. He also demonstrates the first TV broadcast in color.

1938
The Biro brothers invent the ballpoint pen.

1940s
John and Margaret Walson start cable television in Pennsylvania.

1946
Police test the first mobile phones.

1954
Scientists network computers for the U.S. Air Force.

1971
Ray Tomlinson invents e-mail.

Xerox makes the first laser printer.

1975
Kodak experiments with making digital pictures.

1989
Tim Berners-Lee invents the World Wide Web.

1990s
Digital radio stations begin broadcasting in the United States.

High Definition Television (HDTV) becomes popular.

Digital cameras become popular.

2000s
Mobile phones can operate in isolated areas, such as remote parts of Africa.

2001
Apple releases the first iPod.

2006
Western Union sends the final telegraph.

Today
Mobile phones can take pictures; send text messages; play music, games, videos, and more; and they outnumber landlines in some places.

Glossary

ARPANET
a computer network set up in the 1960s by the United States Department of Defense Advanced Research Projects Agency (ARPA)

broadcasts
transmits or sends a radio or television signal over a large area so that many people can receive it

Cold War
the clash of ideas that developed, after World War II, between the United States and the Union of Soviet Socialist Republics

demonstration
the act of showing how something works

develop
to make something over a period of time or to make something better

device
a piece of equipment designed to do a certain task

digital cameras
cameras that use computer technology, instead of film, to take pictures

engineer
a scientist who studies, designs, and builds machines, buildings, and other objects

isolated
far from places with many people

Middle Ages
the period in history from about A.D. 900 until the late 1400s

network
a group of communication devices, such as telephones and computers, that are linked to each other

operator
the person who connects one telephone call to another telephone call

papyrus
a plant that grows in the Nile valley

patent
the ownership rights to an invention that keeps the invention from being copied by others

projected
made an image appear on a surface by shining light through a small, transparent version of the picture

radar
a machine that sends out radio waves and measures the waves when they bounce back

radio waves
electromagnetic waves that have a low frequency and long wavelength. Radio waves are used in both radio and television broadcasts.

rivals
two or more people or companies that try to get the business that only one can have

search engines
Internet sites that enable computer users to search the Internet for specific information

synchronized
happening at the same time

telephone exchange
the equipment that allows telephone calls to be connected to each other

Web browser
computer software that allows users to search for and access information on the World Wide Web

Further Information

Books

Click: A Story About George Eastman. Creative Minds Biography (series). Barbara Mitchell (Carolrhoda Books)

Philo Farnsworth Invents TV. Robbie Readers (series). Russell Roberts (Mitchell Lane)

Web Sites

Federal Communications Commission: Kids Zone
www.fcc.gov/cgb/kidszone/welcome.html

Invention Playhouse: Word Play
inventionatplay.org/playhouse_wordplay.html

Publisher's note to educators and parents: Our editors have carefully reviewed these Web sites to ensure that they are suitable for children. Many Web sites change frequently, however, and we cannot guarantee that a site's future contents will continue to meet our high standards of quality and educational value. Be advised that children should be closely supervised whenever they access the Internet.

Index